WEIRD TRUE FACTS!

PETS!

LIBRARIES NI
WITHDRAWN FROM STOCK

MOIRA BUTTERFIELD

W
FRANKLIN WATTS
LONDON • SYDNEY

Weird True Facts! the boring stuff...

This edition published 2014 by Franklin Watts

Copyright © Franklin Watts 2014
Franklin Watts
338 Euston Road
London NW1 3BH

Franklin Watts Australia
Level 17/207 Kent Street
Sydney, NSW 2000

A CIP catalogue record for this book
is available from the British Library.

Dewey no: 636'.0887

ISBN: 978 1 4451 2967 9

Printed in China.

Franklin Watts is a division of Hachette Children's Books, an Hachette UK company

www.hachette.co.uk

Series editor: Sarah Ridley
Editor in Chief: John C. Miles
Designer: www.rawshock.co.uk/Jason Anscomb
Art director: Jonathan Hair
Picture research: Diana Morris
Picture credits: Alamy Celebrity/Alamy: 29b. Carlo Allegri/Getty Images: 22t. ancroft/
Shutterstock: 25t. Aurora Photos/Alamy: front cover tl. Barcrodt Media/Getty Images: 26t.
Audrey Snider-Bell/Shutterstock: front cover br.Lukas Blazek/Dreamstime: 16b. Joy Brown/
Shutterstock: 11cr. David Crossland/Germany Images/Alamy: 19tr. CSA Images/istockphoto: 15t.
Elias H Debbas/Shutterstock: 10t. Michael De Young/Corbis: 23tr. Dhoxax/Shutterstock: 17tl. Bjorn
Erlandsson/Shutterstock: 24bl. Mary Evans PL/Alamy: 8b. Everett Collection/Rex Features: 20t,
20bl, 20br. Frank Fennema/Shutterstock: 25br. Tim Flack/Getty Images: 26c. goodrich/
Shutterstock: 12b. GH Hart Vikki Hart/Getty Images: 26b. J. Helgason/Shutterstock: 14b. Armin
Hinterwirth/istockphoto: 17b. Hulton Archive/istockphoto: 9br. Hulton-Deutsch/Corbis: 11clb. Eric
Iselée/Shutterstock: front cover bl, 7b, 14tl, 17tc, 23br. Mimmo Jodice/Corbis: 7t. Cathy Keifer/
istockphoto: 18tl. Helko Kiera/Shutterstock: 23bl. kmassman26: 21b. Ksolotis/Dreamstime: 15cl.
Artem Kursin/Shutterstock: 15b. Erik Lam/Shutterstock: 24tl. Alexandra Lande/Shutterstock: 9bc.
Leo Lang/X02157/Reuters/Corbis: front cover bcr, 21c. Lim Tiaw Leong/Shutterstock: 16t.
Clarence Lewis/Shutterstock: 25bl. Chris Lobina/Rex Features: 27t. Mavrixphoto.com: 22br. Mayo
Clinic/Rex Features: 14cr. Dave Napper: 10br. PA/Topham: 11tr. Perig/Shutterstock: 18cr. Armandi
Pharyos/Alamy: 13cr. Michelle Podone/Corbis: 21t. Reuters/Corbis: 8t. Rex Features: 29t. Geoffry
Robinson/Alamy: front cover bc. RT Images/Shutterstock: 28b. Frank Rumpenhorst/epa/Corbis:
27b. Martin Schutt/dpa/Corbis: front cover tr. Alex Segre/Alamy: 10bl. Dmitriy Shironov/
Shutterstock: 19tc. Eric Sohaal/Time Life/Getty Images: 9t. Anna Subbotina/Shutterstock: 12l.
Sygma/Corbis: 23tl. 3drenderings/Shutterstock: 24tr. Trinity Mirror/Mirrorpix /Alamy: 13tl.
Melanie Typaldos/Rex Features: 22bl. Very Olive Photography /Shutterstock: 19br. Steven Vidler/
Eurasia Press/Corbis: 6b. Mike von Burgen/Shutterstock: 19bl. Alfred Wekelo/Shutterstock: 17tr.
Phil Yeomans/Rex Features: 29c. Every attempt has been made to clear copyright.
Should there be any inadvertent omission please apply to the publisher for rectification.

CONTENTS

Ancient animals — Our first furry friends   6

Pets make history — Celebrity companions   8

Hairy heroes — Bravest beasts ever   10

Daft for dogs — Weird stuff for woof-fans   12

Crazy for cats — The pages that purr   14

Fins and fangs - A cuddle-free zone   16

Squeaky secrets — Surprises small and big   18

Pet stars — You were fabulous, darling!   20

Weird pets or weird owners? — It takes all sorts...   22

Yucky pet stuff — Gross zone   24

Pet care — who knew? — Owners go extreme   26

Aaaaaah... babies! — Small surprises   28

Glossary and websites   30

Index   32

OUR FIRST FURRY FRIENDS

People started keeping pets thousands of years ago. Here's some of the history behind our beastie buddies.

A prehistoric cave painting showing a dog helping a human to hunt.

PREHISTORIC POOCHES

Dogs are thought to have been the first ever pets. They were probably descended from tamed wolves and used for hunting. Dog remains found in the Chauvet Cave in Belgium date from over 31,000 years ago. The cave has the first known wall art, too, so we know humans were there at the same time as the dog.

Around 27,000 years ago three dead dogs were buried in what is now the Czech Republic. One of them had a mammoth bone put into its mouth by a human, suggesting some sort of burial ritual for the dogs.

Mummified cats from ancient Egypt, where they were revered as sacred creatures.

Crazy for cats

Nobody knows for sure who tamed the first cat, but it was probably in the area of North Africa. The ancient Egyptians thought that cats were sacred, and they even had their own cat goddess, Bast. Dead cats were mummified and buried in her sacred city.

Cat crime When a pet cat died in ancient Egypt, everyone in the house shaved their eyebrows in mourning.

Cat kidnap It was illegal to export cats from the country, and officials were sent to bring back any cats that had been smuggled out.

DOGS, SNAKES AND APES

The Romans kept all kinds of pets, but they especially liked dogs, and they sometimes gave them grand tombs when they died.

Romans also kept apes as pets, sometimes dressing them up in hats and tunics, and teaching them tricks. One young aristocrat even had trained apes that drove mini chariots pulled by small dogs.

Tame house snakes were a common Roman pet, kept to keep mice and rats down. Emperor Nero (37–68 CE) let his pet snakes glide amongst the guests during banquets.

A wall-painting from a house in Roman Pompeii, showing the god Bacchus (wearing grapes), with a pet dog, a bird and a snake.

Weird pet history

Cool cats Ancient Egyptian Pharaoh Ramesses II (1303–1213 BCE) had a pet lion that he took into battle. Later, Roman Emperor Nero had a pet tigress called Phoebe, which he kept in a golden cage in the garden, and sometimes set on his enemies.

A dog up your sleeve The ancient Chinese bred dogs, such as pugs and Pekingese, to create dogs small enough to fit into the sleeve of a man's robe. Only nobles were allowed to keep them.

CELEBRITY COMPANIONS

The pets on these pages have made their paw marks on history because they belonged to famous people.

US President George W. Bush's pets step off Marine One, the presidential helicopter.

ROYAL DOGS

In 1587 Mary, Queen of Scots (1542-1587), was executed at Fotheringhay Castle in England, for plotting against her cousin, Queen Elizabeth I (1533–1603). After her head had been cut off, witnesses were shocked to see her body move. It turned out that her pet dog, a Skye Terrier, was hiding under her skirts.

Seventeenth-century nobleman Prince Rupert (1619–1682) took Boye, his pet poodle, into battle with him when he fought for the Royalists during the English Civil War (1642–1651). His enemies wrote propaganda accusing the dog of being the devil in disguise – able to catch bullets in its mouth, find treasure and even predict the future.

PRESIDENTS' PETS

US presidents have kept all sorts of pets. Here are just a few notable examples:

'Gators in the garden President Herbert Hoover (1874–1964) had a son who kept two pet alligators in the White House.

Coolidge crowd President Calvin Coolidge (1872–1933) kept many pets, including a donkey, a goose, a bobcat, lion cubs, a pygmy hippo, a wallaby, an antelope and a bear.

Presidential pet names President Theodore Roosevelt (1858–1919) kept many pets including a garter snake called Emily Spinach, a pig called Maude, Jonathan the rat, and a hen called Baron Spreckle.

Mary, Queen of Scots, with a pet dog. She even took one to the execution block with her.

Crazy man, crazy pets:
Twentieth-century artist Salvador Dali liked unusual pets. He once walked an anteater round Paris on a lead, and took his pet ocelot Babu to the best restaurants in town.

Salvador Dali (top left) liked to have himself photographed with crazy pets, such as this bull.

History's craziest pet zoo

A big star Pope Leo X (1475–1521) was given a rare white elephant as a gift in 1514. Its name was Hanno, and it became a big star in parades and important ceremonies.

Guess who's coming to dinner Josephine Bonaparte (1763-1814) was the animal-loving wife of French Emperor Napoleon. She even had a pet orangutan which wore a white dress and ate with her at the dinner table.

Sad song The composer W A Mozart (1756–1791) had a pet starling, which he called 'little fool'. He loved listening to his pet bird sing, and when it died he organised a funeral for his feathery friend.

No rule, no problem Nineteenth-century poet Lord Byron (1788–1824) got round the rule banning dogs in his college rooms. He kept a pet bear instead.

The singing of a pet starling was an inspiration to the composer Mozart.

Lord Byron kept a pet bear when he was a university student.

BRAVEST BEASTS EVER

Many pets have been celebrated for daring or life-saving behaviour. They can't tell their own stories so others have done it for them!

PETS IN STONE

These pets made such a big impression that they were commemorated with a statue.

In 1925 husky Balto led a team of sled dogs over 1,600km (990 miles) from the Alaskan city of Anchorage to the town of Nome, carrying vital serum to prevent an outbreak of the deadly disease diphtheria. The six-day journey made news across the USA. Balto's statue stands in New York's Central Park, USA.

Japanese dog Hachikó waited for nine years at Shibuya Railway Station, hoping his owner would return. Sadly the owner had died, but Hachikó never gave up hope, and his loyalty earned him a statue at the station.

Red Dog has his own statue at Dampier, Australia. He wandered the area in the 1970s, after his owner had died in an accident. He became a local mascot and even had his own bank account.

A statue of Balto, Alaskan dog-hero, in Central Park, New York, USA.

Hachikó, the faithful dog who waited nine years for his master.

A statue of Red Dog, wandering dog hero, in Dampier, Australia.

ANIMAL MEDALLISTS

The British PDSA Dickin Medal is awarded for animal bravery during wartime. Creatures given the medal for their bravery include pigeons, dogs, horses and a cat called Simon.

Simon the cat was on board Royal Navy frigate HMS *Amethyst* in 1949, when it was trapped for more than two months in the Yangtze River in China, under fire from onshore guns. The cat was decorated for catching the rats that threatened the crew's dwindling food supplies.

GI Joe the hero pigeon, wearing his PDSA Dickin medal.

Despite being wounded, Able Seacat Simon hunted rats onboard HMS *Amethyst* (below), and won a medal for his actions.

Chi Chi the Chihuahua barked so much, she helped to save two swimmers in trouble.

GI Joe the pigeon was awarded the Dickin Medal in 1946 for making the most outstanding flight of any US Army pigeon. He flew 32km (20 miles) in twenty minutes to deliver a message that saved hundreds of soldiers.

Upstart the horse got his medal in 1947, for remaining calm and doing his duty despite being showered with glass and debris when a flying bomb exploded in London.

Chihuahua saves drowning woman

A tiny Chihuahua called Chi Chi became a mini heroine in 2008 when she started yelping madly on a beach in North Carolina, USA. Eventually her owners realised that Chi-Chi had seen two elderly ladies struggling in the sea, and the dog's warning led to their rescue.

WEIRD STUFF FOR WOOF-FANS

There are many millions of pet dogs around the world. No wonder there are plenty of unbelievably weird facts, too…

WORLD'S UGLIEST MUTTS

The World's Ugliest Dog Competition is held every year in California, USA, and is regularly won by Chinese Crested Hairless dogs. The champion of champions so far is Sam, who won it a record three times between 2003 and 2005.

Take a look at these crazy-looking dog breeds using the Internet:

Puli – dreadlocks that make it look like a floor mop.

Bedlington Terrier – a dog that looks like a lamb.

Neopolitan Mastiff – a wrinkled face like a deflated balloon.

Bergamasco – dreadlocks that look like felt scales.

Chinese Crested Hairless dogs have almost no hair on their bodies but long tufts on their heads and ankles.

A Bergamasco 'rug' dog, which grows a dreadlock-style coat.

Burtonswood Bossy Boots with television presenter Eamonn Andrews in 1974.

PEDIGREE PETS

Pet dogs that come from top breeders have long, complicated names that may include the name of their birth kennel and their parents. These dogs win prizes at the world's top dog shows. The largest show is Crufts, and here are a few of the winners down the years:

1966 Oakington Puckshill Amber Sunblush
1974 Burtonswood Bossy Boots
1985 Montravia Tommy-Gun
2002 Topscore Contradiction

Believe it or not

Dogs are sacred in some religions but unclean in others.

Dog days In Nepal Hindus worship dogs during the second day of the Festival of Tihar in November.

Dogs beat demons In the ancient Zoroastrian religion, a dog's gaze is considered to be purifying and able to drive off demons.

Happy yappy birthday In China, the second day of the Chinese New Year is considered to be the birthday of all dogs.

A dog being worshipped on Kukur Tihar, the Hindu festival of dogs.

Top Five Totally Weird Dog Facts

1 Barking Sands Beach, in Hawaii, gets its name because its sand sometimes produces a strange sound like a dog barking.

2 Three dogs survived the sinking of the *Titanic*,

3 Surveys suggest that 33% of dog owners leave answerphone messages for their dogs when they are out, and 70% sign their dog's name on greetings cards.

4 The USA is the country with the largest number of dog pets, standing at around 73 million.

5 In parts of South-east Asia dog is eaten, usually

CRAZY FOR CATS

THE PAGES THAT PURR

Next to dogs, cats are the most popular pet in the world. Here are some amazing facts about our furry feline friends.

World's weirdest cats

Check out these unusual cat breeds on the Internet: the Cornish Rex has curly fur and the Sphynx has no fur. The Scottish Fold has flat ears and the Japanese Bobtail has a rabbit tail.

One of the rarest cats in the world glows in the dark. Scientists put a gene from a luminous jellyfish into a cat, to see if it passed the gene onto its kittens. It did, giving birth to glowing babies.

The Sphynx breed of cat has no fur, and big bat-like ears.

Research obtained from cats with glowing jellyfish genes will help fight cat diseases in the future.

GOOD CAT, BAD CAT

Cats can be considered good luck or bad luck, depending on where you live in the world.

Sea safety In the UK, fishermen's wives used to keep a black cat in the house, believing it would bring safety to their husbands.

Money model Japanese homes and shop windows often have a model cat called Maneki Neko on display, to bring good luck and wealth.

Maneki Neko models are not waving. They are beckoning to encourage good luck and wealth.

In medieval Europe, between the 1500s and 1700s, over 175,000 people were put on trial for witchcraft, and either burnt or hanged. One of the signs of being a witch was owning a cat, so thousands of cats were put to death along with their owners.

Why cats? Ancient Scandinavian religion had an important goddess called Freya, who had two cats to help her. When Christianity came to Europe, the early Church officials condemned the old beliefs as wicked, and it's possible that this is why cats came to be associated with witches.

Guilty? Witches were thought to have 'familiars' – demons that hid inside the bodies of animals and helped the witch.

Not guilty? Women living alone were often accused of being witches, and since they often kept cats as pets, it counted as extra evidence against them.

The verdict: Cats were wrongly blamed for all kinds of bad deeds in medieval times, and were also used to condemn their owners to death.

'Get this thing off me...' Fancy dress for cats is available at cat fashion boutiques.

Top Five Totally Weird Cat Facts

1 British scientist Sir Isaac Newton (1643–1727) is known as the first man to discover the laws of gravity, but he also invented the cat flap.

2 Cats sleep for around 70% of the time and spend about 15% of their time cleaning themselves.

3 The oldest cat so far recorded lived to the age of 34.

4 It's possible to buy special clothing for cats, including bridal dresses, tuxedos and angel wings.

5 Cats are left or right pawed, just as humans are left or right handed.

It's even possible to buy knitting patterns for cat sweaters and hats.

A CUDDLE-FREE ZONE

Some pets need to live in tanks full of water, or in terrariums with earth and leaves to replicate the forest floor.

Fishy facts

How stupid are goldfish? It's often said that pet goldfish have a memory of only about 3 seconds, but this was proved wrong by Australian schoolboy scientist Rory Stokes. Over several weeks he trained his goldfish to swim towards a small flashing light 30 seconds before they were fed. Then he switched off the light for a week, and when he switched it back on, the goldfish remembered what to do.

Ugly mug The Ranchu Goldfish is one of the ugliest aquarium fish you could choose. Its eyes and mouth are hidden by the weird lumps and bulges on its head.

Fish for the rich The world's most expensive pet fish is the Platinum Arowana, worth around £63,800 ($100,000).

The Ranchu Goldfish has weird-looking bumps and bulges on its head.

In parts of Asia, freshwater Arowana fish are believed to bring their owners good luck.

SLITHERERS AND STINGERS

Insects, snakes and spiders could be seen as good pets. After all, they're quiet and they don't need to be taken for walks. But without planning and proper care there could be big problems.

Poisonous but popular Tarantulas are popular spider pets, even though they have poisonous fangs and sharp stinging hairs that they fire out when they are upset.

Hungry and hairy Goliath bird-eating spiders make the biggest spider pets, growing up to 28cm (11in) wide, but they don't actually eat birds. They like grasshoppers, crickets and mealworms, with the odd mouse thrown in as a tasty treat.

Treasured scales Pet snakes with beautiful markings are the most expensive. An albino python would set a snake-lover back about £9,600 ($15,000).

A zookeeper poses with a boa constrictor. Many snakes require careful handling.

Cuddling can kill Some snakes, such as boa constrictors, wrap themselves round prey and squeeze it to death. Just occasionally, snake owners have been accidentally choked to death by their boas.

Weird and wonderful

Here are some unusual tank pets that you might not have thought of keeping.

Cute and a good Scrabble word The axolotl is a kind of salamander that lives in water. It can survive for up to 25 years.

Guess the pet Would you like a sea mouse as a pet, or perhaps a christmas tree? These are both species of marine worms that you can keep in an aquarium.

Axolotls have to be kept on their own because they fight, often biting off each other's toes.

SURPRISES SMALL & BIG

Singing mice, holy rats and giant dog-sized rabbits are all to be found in the world of extreme mini pets.

Rodent zone

Rats and mice make friendly entertaining pets. Rats, in particular, are quite intelligent and can be taught simple tricks such as paw-shaking. They've even been trained to sniff out land mines.

Rats rule at the Karni Mata Temple in India where the Hindu rat goddess is worshipped. Worshippers visit the temple, where 20,000 rats live, in the hope of being blessed by the goddess.

When a male mouse meets a mate it sings! It squeaks in a high pitch that humans can't hear, but when scientists recorded the noise and played it at a lower pitch, they discovered it sounded just like birdsong.

Although this cute picture of rats is faked, rodents are in fact very clever and can be taught to do many tricks in real life.

Rats are given plenty of treats at the Karni Mata Temple in India.

Five weird ratty mousy facts

1 Rats can't vomit.

2 In China, rats are a symbol of prosperity.

3 The word 'mouse' comes from ancient Sanskrit, meaning 'thief'.

4 Mice have a soft skull, which helps them to squeeze through very small holes.

EXTREME RABBITS

The largest rabbit breeds can grow as big as dogs. One of the largest, the German Giant, can grow up to 1m (39in) tall and tips the scales at over 7kg (15.5lb).

Angora rabbits have lots of fur, which can be used to make extra-soft knitting wool. When the angoras are brushed, they look like big woolly balls.

Rabbits have a great sense of smell, many times better than a human. They can't fart or burp.

Rabbits twitch their noses to smell their surroundings for food or danger.

One big bunny – German Giant rabbits grow as big as dogs.

Guinea pigs and hamsters – Shock warning!

If you love guinea pigs or hamsters, you might find a few upsetting shocks in this section, so brace yourself…

Guinea guzzlers Guinea pigs come from South America, where they are reared for food. Peruvian families eat millions of guinea pigs a year.

Guinea supergiant The prehistoric fossil of a giant guinea pig-like animal was found in Venezuela, South America. It was given the nickname 'guinea-zilla' because it was the size of a large cow.

Banned! Hamsters are banned in Australia and New Zealand in case they start to breed in the wild, where their numbers could quickly get out of hand.

Hamsters are banned from Australia and New Zealand.

Roasted guinea pigs on sale in a South American market.

YOU WERE FABULOUS, DARLING!

Talented animals can become big celebrities, with their own agents and fans.

Lassie was one of the world's most famous movie stars in the 1940s and 1950s.

Movie magic
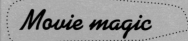

Pets with star-quality can now be signed up to acting school to help them follow in the paw (or hoof) prints of Hollywood superstars.

Top dog Lassie became the world's most famous movie dog character, appearing in many Hollywood movies and TV shows from 1943 onwards. In fact, many different dogs played the character, and though Lassie was female, the doggie actors were all male. The film directors preferred male dogs because they are bigger and have thicker coats.

Stuffed superstar Cowboy actor Roy Rogers (1911–1998) made over 80 western movies with his world-renowned horse, Trigger. When Trigger died he was stuffed, and in 2010 he was auctioned for $266,500 (£166,800).

When Trigger died he was stuffed, standing in his famous rearing pose.

Trigger appeared in many cowboy movies with his rider, Roy Rogers.

ROY ROGERS
KING OF THE COWBOYS

'TRIGGER'
SMARTEST HORSE IN THE MOVIES

HANDS ACROSS THE BORDER
A REPUBLIC PICTURE

RUTH TERRY
GUINN "BIG BOY" WILLIAMS

WHAT CAN YOU TEACH PETS?

Cockatoos, pigs, dogs and horses seem to be the best pets to train.

Doggie dancing Dog freestyle dancing competitions have become part of many modern dog shows. Owners dance in routines along with their dogs, to showcase their pet's obedience and clever tricks such as rolling over and spinning.

Dog freestyle dancing competitions are becoming popular worldwide.

Porkie performers Pigs are as clever as dogs when it comes to learning tricks, and they sometimes perform in piggie display teams – even show-jumping, dancing, slam-dunking basketballs, riding scooters and skateboards.

Can fleas pull carts? Travelling flea circuses were once popular animal entertainments. Fleas were tied by gold wire to tiny objects, such as mini carts or fairground wheels, and spectators could watch them moving. In reality, the fleas weren't trained. They were just trying to get away.

Birds on bicycles Cockatoos and macaws can be trained to say words and also to do tricks such as riding bicycles on tightropes, which makes them ideal bird performers. In Australia talking cockatoos that have escaped from their owners have joined up with wild bird flocks and apparently passed on their word skills to young wild birds, who've learnt to say phrases such as 'what's happening?' and 'hello there'.

Macaws are good at performing in public. This one is riding a bird-sized unicycle on a tightrope.

JIM THE WONDER DOG
1925 — 1937

A winner who picked winners

Jim the Wonder Dog was a big pet celebrity in the 1930s, and has his own park and statue in the town of Marshall, Missouri, USA. Jim could apparently forecast baseball match results and horserace winners, and correctly predicted the winner of the Kentucky Derby seven times in a row.

IT TAKES ALL SORTS... Here are some of the most unusual pets ever, along with the unusual owners who love them.

Crazy pet true stories

A happy ending In 1969 John Rendall and Ace Bourke bought a lion cub at Harrods store in London, UK. They named him Christian and used to take him for rides round town in their car, but as he grew bigger they decided to release him into a wildlife reserve in Kenya. A year later his former owners visited, and in recent years film of the touching reunion became a massive YouTube hit.

Pet passenger Canadian Jim Sautner has an 826kg buffalo called Bailey Junior as a family pet. Bailey rides with Jim in a specially-adapted car, and even watches TV with the family.

Internet pet When Melanie Typaldos went on holiday to Venezuela, she saw giant guinea pig-like capybaras in the wild. On returning to Texas, she arranged to adopt one, and called it Caplin Rous. Caplin became a celebrity and even had its own blog and daily tweets, before it died in 2011.

Buffalo Bailey Junior shares the kitchen with his owner, Jim Sautner.

Lizard man Hollywood herpetoculturist (lizard owner) Henry Lizardlover was so fascinated by his pet lizards, he changed his name.

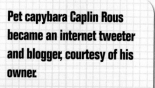

Pet capybara Caplin Rous became an internet tweeter and blogger, courtesy of his owner.

Henry Lizardlover makes tiny furniture and props such as bicycles for his pet lizards.

Tiger cubs make cute pets until they grow up and get less friendly.

WILD ANIMALS NEXT DOOR

It's thought there are between 10,000 and 15,000 tigers being kept as pets in the USA, many more than are left in the wild. There are regular deaths and maulings when pets turn on their owners, and so laws have been tightened up to try to limit the sale of tigers to those who are not experts.

Hollywood actor Nicolas Cage owned two King Cobra snakes, and a bottle of serum to combat their deadly poison. When frightened neighbours complained, he donated them to a local zoo.

The crazy pet shop

Someone somewhere keeps one of these!

Skunk Having a pet skunk sounds stinky, but skunk owners have the scent gland of their pets removed, so they don't spray the foul-smelling liquid that wild skunks produce.

Anteater Angela Goodwin draws surprised looks when she takes her two pet anteaters, Pua and Stewie, for walks. They like to raid her fridge for their favourite food – blue cheese.

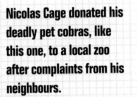

Nicolas Cage donated his deadly pet cobras, like this one, to a local zoo after complaints from his neighbours.

US pet owner Angela Goodwin has pet anteaters that she takes for walks.

GROSS ZONE

Pets are loveable and interesting, of course, but they can also be disgusting, so be warned. This page might just turn you off your animal friends!

Pets have gross habits for a reason. What's your excuse?

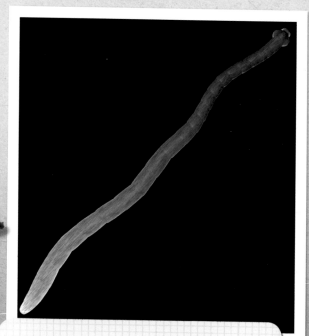

An intestinal tapeworm, just one of the many unpleasant parasites that dogs can pick up.

The pet poo files

Poo rolling Dogs sometimes like to roll in other animals' smelly poo, much to their owners' disgust. This weird habit could be a hangover from ancient times, when dogs may have done it to disguise their own scent when they were out hunting.

Poo power Scientists are looking at ways of recycling pet poo by converting it into methane gas to use as fuel.

MYSTERY VISITORS

Occasionally your pet might have a few unwelcome guests, and could even pass them on to you. Dangers such as these can be avoided if you look after a pet properly.

• Dogs can pick up parasites such as ear mites, hookworms, roundworms, heartworms, tapeworms, ticks and whipworms.

• Humans can catch a very nasty illness called toxoplasmosis from a germ found in cat poo.

• Reptiles and amphibians such as turtles, lizards and frogs can pass on the salmonella germ, which can cause serious illness in humans.

DAY IN THE LIFE OF A FLEA

Here's the life story of a pet flea, the most common unwelcome pet guest.

The big jump Fleas will jump onto warm-blooded animals such as cats and dogs. They can leap up to 200 times their own body length, the best jumping performance of any animal.

Dinner The flea bites its host and sucks their blood. Meanwhile the flea's spit causes itching on the skin.

New babies Female fleas lay eggs on the host's skin, which drop off and hatch into tiny larvae that gradually develop into new fleas.

Hungry again When the new fleas sense the warmth and vibration of an animal going by, they hop onboard!

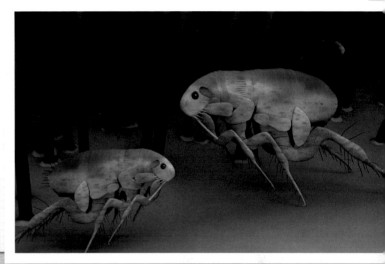

A computer-enhanced magnification of common fleas living on an animal host.

Why be so gross?

Dogs lick people as a sign of submission. In a pack of dogs, the lesser dogs lick the leader.

Dogs sniff each other's backsides because a dog's bottom contains anal scent glands that produce a powerful scent. Each dog will have its own smell, so the backside-sniffing is a way for dogs to get to know each other.

Dogs spray urine in places to mark that they were there, like a sort of smelly version of graffiti. Other passing dogs will smell the scent.

Dogs get to know each other by sniffing.

When a dog pees on something it's leaving the message 'I was here' for other dogs.

OWNERS GO EXTREME

Some owners will go to amazing lengths and expense to look after their beloved pets and ensure they look their best.

Poodle-saurus – an entry at a creative dog-grooming competition in the United States.

Looking good

Creative dog-grooming contests are popular in the USA, and now in other parts of the world, too. Owners bring their dogs onstage and then take part in a timed competition to transform their dogs into something unusual, using dye and props. There are big cash prizes for the winners.

It's possible to buy all sorts of pet outfits, including lots of unusual fancy dress costumes, and even a bottom-hole coverer for your cat or dog, decorated with a butterfly or a smiley face. There are also decorated dog nappies for pooches who are prone to embarrassing accidents.

Dogs in space – another creative but super-weird entry, with a Bedlington Terrier this time.

Dogs can even marry each other, dressed in wedding outfits.

Lucky pooches get pampered at the Canyon View Ranch country estate for dogs, in California, USA.

NOTHING BUT THE BEST

The best address There are lots of luxury pet homes on the market, including canine mansions that cost thousands, and they can include such luxuries as a spa, a plasma TV, temperature-controlled beds and even pet iris-recognition software that stops any other animals getting in.

Flush next to fish The toilet aquarium is a tank that fits behind a toilet, so you can see fish swimming as you go. It may look like an integral part of the toilet, but in reality it's separate, so the fish don't get flushed.

Luxury beastie breaks You can treat your dog or cat to its own luxury holiday by checking it into a luxury pet hotel. Guests get their own rooms, and services on offer may include a mini bar containing yummy pet treats, a snuggly robe, chef-prepared food and room service.

Food for furry friends

Pet food was first sold in the early 1800s, but nowadays it is much healthier. It's even possible to have your pet's DNA sequenced, and then order bespoke pet foods designed on the results.

Owners can now go to dog and cat food cooking classes, to produce their own delicious homemade pet food. Recipes available online include doggie birthday cake, doggie bad breath biscuits, canine cookies, dog gravy and 'frosty paws' doggie ice cream. Recipes for cats include crispy fish dinner, cat jelly, cat wraps, fish pudding and kitty biscuits.

A luxury dog mansion — for the pet who has everything.

SMALL SURPRISES

Baby pets come in all shapes, sizes and colours, some of them surprising…

Mothers with the most

In 2005, a Neapolitan Mastiff gave birth to 24 puppies, a new dog record. Her owners were expecting a maximum of ten, so it came as a big surprise. Twenty of the puppies survived.

In 1970 a Burmese cat called Tarawood Antigone gave birth to a record 19 kittens, 15 of whom survived. Fourteen were male, and one was female.

ANIMAL ALLSORTS

Hybrid animals are the young resulting from parents of different related species, and can sell for large sums of money as unusual 'designer' pets.

Dog duo There are many types of 'cross-breed' dog. Cross-breeds are given a name that mixes the breed names of their parents. A few examples include:

Bogle – Beagle and boxer

Cockapoo – Cocker Spaniel and poodle

Dorgi – Dachshund and corgi

Hug – Husky and pug

Papijack – Papillon and Jack Russell

Bogles combine the inquisitive nature of a beagle with the temperament of a boxer.

Cockapoos make good family pets.

Cloning your kitty

Every individual creature has its own DNA, material inside every living cell which provides information triggering the way that the body grows and changes. Cloning means using DNA from an animal to create a baby which is a copy.

The first ever cloned cat was called Copycat, created by scientists in Texas, USA. The first cat to be commercially cloned was Little Nicky, who cost his owner £26,000 ($50,000). He was created from the DNA of her much-loved previous cat.

Little Nicky, the first-ever commercially cloned cat.

A Toyger cat, bred to have a striped tiger-like coat.

Rare riders Horse-owners who want something more unusual can go for one of the three 'zebroids', with zebra in the mix. Zebroids make for interesting pets, but they may also be bad-tempered and difficult to handle.

A zorse is a cross between a horse and a zebra.

A zony is a cross between a pony and a zebra.

A zedonk is a cross between a donkey and a zebra.

A zorse, a rare cross between a horse and a zebra.

Cat collection Domestic cats are sometimes crossed with small wild cats and carefully bred to create unusual coats. Examples include the Toyger, bred to have a striped coat, and the Mokave, which has a spotted coat and ancestors that include a lynx and an Asian Leopard cat.

A Toyger, with stripes like a tiger.

A Mokave, with spots like a leopard.

A Cheetoh, a cross-breed between a Bengal and an Ocicat.

Amphibian A type of animal that spends time both in water and on land, such as a frog or a salamander.

Angora A type of rabbit with lots of soft hair.

Aquarium A tank filled with water, for keeping underwater creatures.

Arowana A type of freshwater fish prized by aquarium owners.

Axolotl A type of salamander that can be kept in an aquarium.

Bacteria Tiny one-celled organism which can sometimes be harmful to humans and pets.

Bast An ancient Egyptian cat goddess. Sacred cats lived in the goddess's temple in the town of Bastet.

Bedlington A type of terrier dog with pale curly fur, making it look rather like a lamb.

Bergamasco A type of dog with long matted felt-like fur.

Boa constrictor A type of snake that squeezes its prey to death.

Canine Relating to dogs.

Capybara A large guinea pig-like creature from South America.

Cross-breed A creature whose parents are two different breeds of the same animal type (such as two different breeds of dog, for instance).

Crufts The world's biggest dog show, held in the UK every year.

Dickin Medal A medal awarded for animal bravery, presented by the PDSA (People's Dispensary for Sick Animals) in the UK.

DNA Material inside every living cell which provides information triggering the way that body cells grow and change.

Familiar A mythical demon supposedly disguised as a creature living with a witch.

Feline Relating to cats.

German Giant A very large type of rabbit.

Gland A part of the body that produces a secretion – a substance that is used by the body. Animal glands produce such things as scent which other animals can recognise, or oil to keep fur waterproof.

Grooming Looking after a pet's appearance, including washing and brushing fur.

Herpetoculturist Someone who keeps reptiles or amphibians in captivity.

Hybrid A cross between two related types of animal.

Iris-recognition software A computer chip that records the unique pattern of the coloured part of the eye – the iris.

Karni Mata A temple in India, sacred to rats.

Litter A group of animal babies born together.

Maneki Neko The Japanese figure of a cat with one paw raised, thought to be a lucky charm.

Muricide The killing of rats or mice.

Parasite A creature that exists by living and feeding on another living creature.

Pedigree The record of a pet's ancestors.

Pekingese A type of dog first bred in ancient China.

Pug A type of small dog first kept in ancient China, for nobles.

Python A type of snake from Australia, Asia or Africa.

Reptile A type of animal that is cold-blooded and has a scaly skin.

Simulation A fake version of something, such as a robot pet.

Species A specific group of animals.

Superstition An old belief not based on fact.

Tapeworm A type of worm that lives inside the guts of animals.

Terrarium A container for earth, plants and animals.

Toxoplasmosis A harmful disease than can be caught by humans, from germs found in some pet droppings.

Zebroid A cross between a zebra and a horse, donkey or pony.

WEB PETS

There are many pet care and pet fact sites on the Internet. Here are a few fun examples:

http://www.greyfriarsbobby.co.uk
The stories of famous heroic dogs from around the world.

http://www.animalsinwar.org.uk
Stories of famous animals in wartime.

http://www.cat-world.com.au/cat-world-records
Amazing cat record-breakers, including the cat who survived the highest fall, the cat who has caught the most mice and the owner with the most cats.

http://www.dogbreedinfo.com
A list of all dog breeds, along with information.

http://exoticpets.about.com
Lots of information about unusual pets.

http://www.petplace.com/
All sorts of information about keeping pets of all kinds.

Note to parents and teachers

Every effort has been made by the Publishers to ensure that the websites in this book are suitable for children, that they are of the highest educational value, and that they contain no inappropriate or offensive material. However, because of the nature of the Internet, it is impossible to guarantee that the contents of these sites will not be altered. We strongly advise that Internet access is supervised by a responsible adult.

alligators 8
anteaters 9, 23
apes 7
axolotl 17

Bailey Junior (buffalo) 22
Balto (dog) 10
Bast 6
bears 8, 9
birds 7, 9, 11, 21
   cockatoo 21
   macaw 21
   pigeon 11
   starling 9
Bonaparte, Josephine 9
Bourke, Ace 22
bulls 9
Burtonswood Bossy Boots 13
Bush, George W. 8
Byron, Lord 9

Cage, Nicolas 23
Caplin Rous (capybara) 22
cat flap 15
cats 6, 7, 11, 14–15, 24, 25, 26, 29
   cloning 29
   cross-breeds 29
   mummified 6
   cat breeds,
      Burmese 28
      Cornish Rex 14
      Japanese Bobtail 14
      Scottish Fold 14
      Sphynx 14
      Toyger 29
Chi Chi (dog) 11
China, ancient 7
Christian (lion) 22
clothing, pet 7, 9, 15, 26
Coolidge, President Calvin 8
Crufts Dog Show 13

Dali, Salvador 9
Dickin Medal 11
dogs 6, 7, 8, 9, 12–13, 19, 20, 21,
   24, 25, 27, 28
   cross-breeds 28
   dancing competitions 21
   dog-grooming contests 26
   pedigree 13
   scent/sniffing 24, 25

dog breeds,
   Basset Hound 26
   Bedlington Terrier 12, 26
   Bergamasco 12
   Bogle 28
   Chihuahua 11
   Chinese Crested Hairless 12
   Cockapoo 28
   husky 10, 28
   Neopolitan Mastiff 12, 28
   Pekingese 7
   poodle 8, 26, 28
   pug 7, 28
   Puli 12
   St Bernard 13
   Skye Terrier 8
donkeys 8, 29

Egypt, ancient 6, 7
elephants 9
Emperor Nero 7

fish 16, 27
   Arowana 16
   goldfish 16
fleas 21, 25
food, pet 27

GI Joe (pigeon) 11
Goodwin, Angela 23
guinea pigs 19, 22

Hachikō (dog) 10
hamsters 19
HMS Amethyst 11
homes, luxury pet 27
Hoover, President Herbert 8
horses 11, 20, 21, 29
hybrids 28
hygiene, pet 24

insects 17

Jim the Wonder Dog 21

Karni Mata Temple 18
kittens 14, 28

Lassie (dog) 20
lions 7, 8, 22
Little Nicky (cat) 29
Lizardlover, Henry 22
lizards 22, 24

Maneki Neko 14
Mary, Queen of Scots 8
mice 7, 17, 18
movies 20
Mozart, W A 9

Newton, Sir Isaac 15

ocelots 9
orangutans 9

PDSA 11
Pharaoh Ramesses 7
pigs 8, 21
poo 24
Pope Leo X 9
Prince Rupert 8
puppies 28

rabbits 18, 19
   angora 18
   German Giant 19
rats 7, 8, 11, 18
Red Dog 10
religion 13, 15, 18
Rendall, John 22
Rogers, Roy 20
Romans, ancient 7
Roosevelt, President Theodore 8

Sautner, Jim 22
Simon (the cat) 11
skunks 23
snakes 7, 8, 17, 23
   King Cobras 23
spiders 17
statues, pet 10, 21
Stokes, Rory 16
superstitions 14, 15

tigers 7, 23
tricks, teaching pets 18, 21
Trigger (the horse) 20
Typaldos, Melanie 22

witchcraft 15
World's Ugliest Dog Competition 12
worms, marine 17

zebroids 29